The Living Room, Rearranged

Yael Grunseit

Harbor Editions
Small Harbor Publishing

Much of this work was created on the stolen land of the Gadigal people of the Eora Nation. Yael Grunseit and Harbor Editions pay their respects to elders past, present, and emerging. Sovereignty was never ceded.

Always was, always will be Aboriginal land.

The Living Room, Rearranged

Cover art by Jackie Ruttner
Cover design by Ilan Galanti
Book layout by Claire Eder

THE LIVING ROOM, REARRANGED
YAEL GRUNSEIT
ISBN 978-1-957248-09-7
Harbor Editions,
an imprint of Small Harbor Publishing

For Rolf

Contents

The Living Room, Rearranged

א. To Desire

"Rav said, and some say it was Rabbi Yohanan who said: Woe, woe. It is this, i.e., the evil inclination for idol worship, that destroyed the Temple, and burned its Sanctuary, and murdered all the righteous ones, and caused the Jewish people to be exiled from their land. And it still dances among us, i.e., it still affects us. Didn't You give it to us solely for the purpose of our receiving reward for overcoming it? We do not want it, and we do not want its reward. We are prepared to forgo the potential rewards for overcoming the evil inclination as long as it departs from us."

—Yoma 69b: 6. Babylonian Talmud.

The Babylonian Talmud is a compilation of rabbinic commentaries, the Mishnah and the Babylonian Gemara. It is the foundation of Jewish law and tradition. Each page contains many interpretations.

עין משפט נר מצוה

[illegible]

אין ישיבה בעזרה אלא למלכי בית דוד בלבד שנאמר ויבא המלך דוד וישב לפני ה' כדאמר רב חסדא בעזרת נשים הכא נמי בעזרת נשים והיכא איתמר דרב חסדא אהא [א] א) מיתיבי דתניא היכן קורין בו בעזרה ראב"י אומר בהר הבית שנאמר ויקרא בו לפני הרחוב אשר לפני שער המים ואמר רב חסדא בעזרת נשים ויברך עזרא את ה' האלהים הגדול מאי גדול אמר רב יוסף אמר רב שגדלו בשם המפורש רב גידל אמר ברוך ה' אלהי ישראל מן העולם ועד העולם אמר ליה אביי [ב] לרב דימי ודילמא שגידלו בשם המפורש א"ל אין אומרים שם המפורש בגבולים ולא א) והכתיב [ג] ויעמוד עזרא הסופר על מגדל עץ אשר עשו לדבר ואמר רב גידל שגדלו בשם המפורש הוראת שעה היתה [ד] ויצעקו אל ה' אלהים בקול גדול מאי אמור אמר רב ואיתימא ר' יוחנן בייא בייא היינו האי דאחרביה למקדשא וקליה להיכליה וקטלינהו לכולהו צדיקי ואגלינהו לישראל מארעהון ועדיין מרקד בינן כלום יהבתיה לן אלא לקבולי ביה אגרא לא איהו בעינן ולא אגריה בעינן נפל להו פיתקא מרקיעא דהוה כתב בה אמת אמר רב חנינא שמע מינה חותמו של הקב"ה אמת אותיבו בתעניתא תלתא יומין ותלתא לילואתא מסרוהו ניהליהו נפק אתא כי ג) גוריא דנורא מבית קדשי הקדשים אמר להו נביא לישראל היינו יצרא דעבודת כוכבים שנאמר ויאמר זאת הרשעה בהדי דתפסוה ליה אשתמיט ביניתא ממזייא ורמא קלא ואזל קליה ארבע מאה פרסי אמרו היכי נעביד דילמא חס ושלום מרחמי עליה מן שמיא אמר להו נביא שדיוהו בדודא דאברא וחפיוהו לפומיה באברא דאברא משאב שאיב קלא שנאמר ויאמר זאת הרשעה וישלך אותה אל תוך האיפה וישלך את אבן העופרת אל פיה אמרו הואיל ועת רצון הוא נבעי רחמי איצרא דעבירה בעו רחמי ואמסר בידייהו אמר להו חזו דאי קטליתו ליה להההוא ג) כליא עלמא חבשוהו תלתא יומי ובעו ביעתא בת יומא ד) בכל ארץ ישראל ולא אשתכח אמרי היכי נעביד נקטליה כליא עלמא ניבעי רחמי אפלגא פלגא ברקיעא לא יהבי כחלינהו לעיניה ושבקוהו ואהני דלא מיגרי ביה לאיניש בקריבתה במערבא מתנו הכי רב גידל אמר ה) גדול שגדלו בשם המפורש ורב מתנא אמר האל הגדול הגבור והנורא והא דרב מתנא [ה] מטייא לדרבי יהושע בן לוי דאמר רבי יהושע בן לוי למה נקרא שמן אנשי כנסת הגדולה שהחזירו עטרה ליושנה אתא משה אמר האל הגדול הגבור והנורא אתא ירמיה ואמר נכרים מקרקרין בהיכלו איה נוראותיו לא אמר נורא אתא דניאל אמר נכרים משתעבדים בבניו איה גבורותיו לא אמר גבור אתו אינהו ואמרו אדרבה זו היא ו) גבורת גבורתו שכובש את [ו] יצרו שנותן ארך אפים לרשעים ואלו הן נוראותיו שאלמלא מוראו של הקב"ה היאך אומה אחת יכולה להתקיים בין האומות ורבנן היכי עבדי הכי ועקרי תקנתא דתקין משה אמר רבי אלעזר מתוך שיודעין בהקב"ה שאמתי הוא לפיכך לא כיזבו בו: וקורא אחרי מות ואך בעשור: ורמינהו מדלגין בנביא ואין מדלגין בתורה לא קשיא כאן בכדי שיפסיק התורגמן כאן בכדי שלא יפסיק התורגמן והא עלה קתני מדלגין בנביא ואין מדלגין בתורה ועד כמה מדלג בכדי שלא יפסיק התורגמן הא בתורה כלל כלל לא אמר אביי לא קשיא כאן בענין אחד כאן בשני ענינין והתניא מדלגין בתורה בענין אחד ובנביא בשני ענינין כאן וכאן בכדי שלא יפסיק התורגמן ואין מדלגין מנביא לנביא ובנביא של שנים עשר מדלגין ובלבד

רש"י

אין ישיבה בעזרה. דכתיב לעמוד לשרת (דברים יח) העומדים שם לפני ה' (שם) ולא מצינו בה ישיבה: **אלא למלכי בית דוד שנאמר ויבא המלך דוד וישב וגו'.** כשאמר לו נתן הנביא אתה לא תבנה הבית כי ימלאו ימיך וגו': **ויברך עזרא וגו'.** כההוא ענינא דויקרא לפני הרחוב כתיב ברוך ה' אלהים וגו' כך תיקנו באותו היום לומר במקדש בסוף כל ברכה וברכה כדאמרינן במסכת תענית (דף טז:): **בגבולין.** כל חוץ לעזרה קרי גבולין: **בייא בייא.** לשון צעקה וקובלנא: **האי דאחרביה לבית המקדש.** מבקשין רחמים שימסר בידם יצר הרע של עבודת כוכבים: **לקבולי אגרא.** שנכוף אותו ונקבל שכר: **פיתקא.** כתב: **אמת.** כלומר מסכים אני עמכם: **אמר להו נביא.** זכריה בן עדו: **ביניתא.** שיער: **בדודא דאברא.** בסיר של עופרת: **זאת הרשעה.** וישלך אותה אל תוך האיפה וגו' (ויתן) את אבן העופרת אל פיה: **שאיב קלא.** נכנס הקול לתוך העופרת ואינו יוצא ממנו: **כליא עלמא.** יכלה העולם שלא תהא פריה ורביה: **ביעתא בת יומא.** ביצה הנולדה בו ביום לפי שפסק החימום מן המעים ואפילו אותן שעיברה התרנגולת כבר אין מתבשלין במעיה: **לפלגא.** שיהא שולט באדם ליזקק לאשתו ולא לאחרת: **כחלינהו.** שימו את עיניו ע"י כחול: **האל הגדול הגבור והנורא.** אשר לא ישא פנים: **עובדי כוכבים מקרקרים בהיכלו.** שראה שרי נבוכדנצר נכנסין להיכל ומריעים בו ככל רצונם: **לא אמר נורא.** בפרשת הנה חנמאל כתיב עושה חסד לאלפים ומשלם עון אבות אל חיק בניהם אחריהם האל הגדול והגבור ה' צבאות שמו (ירמיה לב): **דניאל לא אמר גבור.** בתפלתו בספרו (דניאל ט): **עובדי כוכבים משתעבדים בבניו.** זה שבעים שנה: **זו היא גבורתו.** שכובש יצרו כל השנים הללו שנשתעבדו בהן ומאריך אפו על כל הגזירות שגוזרים על בניו: **ואלו הן נוראותיו שאלמלא מוראו וכו'.** מן יום החורבן אתה למד נוראותיו שכל האומות נאספו להשמידם ונתקיימו מהן: **ורבנן.** ירמיה ודניאל: **שהוא אמתי.** מסכים על האמת ואינו אוהב את השקר: **כאן בכדי שיפסיק התורגמן.** הא דקתני אין מדלגין בפרשה הרחוקה מזה שקודם שגולל ספר תורה עד מקום הדילוג יפסיק התורגמן המתרגם פסוק שקרא הקורא ונמצאו צבור יושבין ומצפין אין זה כבוד צבור אבל אך בעשור סמוכה היא לאחרי מות ויכול לגלול שם קודם שיפסיק התורגמן: **בענין אחד.** כגון הכא ששתי הפרשיות מדברות בענין יוה"כ מדלגין ובכדי שלא יפסיק התורגמן והא דקתני דאפילו בכדי שלא יפסיק נמי לא ידלג בשני ענינים לפי שדברי תורה היא אזהרות ועונשין ומצות וצריך שיכנסו בלב השומעין וכשאדם יוצא משיטה ו) לשיטה אחרת אינו נוח להתבונן: **והסגיא.** בניחותא:

תוספות

אין ישיבה בעזרה. פירשתי לעיל בפרק שני (דף כה.) גבי זקן יושב במערבה:

ועד כמה הוא מדלג בכדי שלא יפסיק התורגמן. לא בעי לשנויי דאתורה קאי משום דקתני אין מדלגין בתורה הדר קא מפרש ועד כמה מותר לדלג בתורה בכדי שלא יפסיק התורגמן והא דאמרי ברישא בכדי שיפסיק התורגמן וי"ל דאין הכי נמי דהוה מצי לשנויי הכי אלא אביי מתרץ לו האמת כאן בענין אחד כאן בשני ענינין כדתניא וכו':

מסורת הש"ס

[illegible]

הגהות הב"ח

[illegible]

הגהות הגר"א

[illegible]

הגהות מהר"ב רנשבורג

[illegible]

תום' ישנים

[illegible]

תורה אור השלם

[illegible]

...אלהיכם הוא אלהי האלהים ואדני האדנים האל הגדל הגבר והנורא אשר לא ישא פנים ולא יקח שחד: דברים י יז

גליון הש"ס

גמרא ויצעקו וכו' ויזעקו בקול גדול אל ה' אלהיהם כצ"ל:

מוסף רש"י

הובא בסוף המסכת

רבינו חננאל

אין ישיבה בעזרה אלא למלכי בית דוד בלבד. שנאמר, ויבא המלך דוד וישב לפני ה'. ושנינן כדאמר רב חסדא כי עזרא דכתיב ביה ויקרא בו לפני הרחוב אשר לפני שער המים, בעזרת הנשים קרא. כך כהן גדול בעזרת הנשים היה קורא ומאתר לו לישב שם. כתיב ויברך עזרא את ה' אלהים, מאי אמר אמר רב יוסף ברוך המבורך. א"ל אביי לרב דימי איפא שבירכו בשם המפורש א"ל אין אומרים שם המפורש בגבולים כלומר אין מברכין בשם המפורש חוץ לעזרה. ולא, והכתיב ויעמוד עזרא הסופר על מגדל עץ אשר עשו לדבר. ואמר רב יהודה אמר רב שגידלו בשם המפורש. והנה זה בגבולין הוה. ושנינן הוראת שעה היתה. דכתיב ויצעקו בקול גדול אל ה' האלהים. מאי אמרו, אר"י ואיתימא רבי נתי בייא בייא כו'. רב מתנא אמר ויברך עזרא את ה' האלהים הגדול שגידלו בשם המפורש [illegible]

תוספות ישנים

[illegible]

The donkey

stood in my kitchen. A thick scribble of almost blinding white light coloured in her head, neck, torso and two legs. She always stood side-on and had no eyes or hooves. She grew and shrunk

as she pleased, not subject to any outline. I opened the fridge and pulled out a carrot while my eyes remained fixated on her. I didn't want to look away even for a moment. I pointed the carrot towards her head, she obviously refused. I wanted to pat the donkey but I was too scared. I wanted to talk, but I didn't. We didn't need to talk. At first I thought she was here to celebrate my

unwavering belief in her powers. Then I realised this was more of an intervention. Maybe she'd make me fast for a month or banish all my nice clothes so

that I could be free from unneces sary desires. Maybe she was going to stick around, always by my side to guide me. I needed her guidance. The donkey commanded me to eat her. Strangle her to death, really push my thumbs deep into her esophagus. Then

cut up her

body with a cleaver. I would need to drive to my mum's house and grab her's. Once disassembled she wanted me to fry her in a pan with olive oil, salt and pepper. She made me picture myself slobbering while gnawing on her leg, letting her greasy light drip down my chin. She instructed me to consume all of her, to let my stomach balloon and growl from fullness. She trotted a step to the left. She turned on my stove. I waited a moment, maybe she was joking, maybe it was a test. She shamed me for thinking I was like Abraham. I went to wrap my hands around her girthy neck that swirled with static scribbles. I had no problem following her instructions. I would do whatever she asked. She was warm like I expected. I could feel a skin tag under my right middle finger like the one on my own neck. I rested my head on hers and kept a firm grip, wanting to impress her with my strength. After thirty seconds, I heard some rustling coming from my room. I told myself it was probably nothing, but I knew that it wasn't nothing. It was probably someone trying to break in. Maybe my neighbour had seen the donkey through the window above my kitchen sink, and in five seconds Dan would be behind me with a machete, and he'd fling the machete at my back. Maybe it was Ruth, and I'd fall to my knees screaming, clutching my chest as blood dribbled into my hands while she cackled and kicked my head to the floor. Three seconds now and Ruth would be a metre behind me drooling because she was going to eat my donkey. Two seconds and my back was tingling. I could tell Dan and Ruth were both behind me about to hurl their machetes at my skull, so I released my hands from around her neck. She breathed heavily. No one was behind me. I walked to my room and opened my door. I checked under my bed, my desk, in each drawer, under my bed again, in my jewelry box, in each drawer again. Nothing was there, obviously. I ran back to the donkey and flung my hands around her neck. Thirty seconds passed and I heard more rustling from my room.

I wish I liked her more 69b

Liat left a blue sticky note that said "Truth" in the centre of my laptop screen. Last time she left a sticky note it said "you're beautiful xx." I can't tell if her notes are ironic. When I ask, she laughs and kisses me. We don't message or call often but when we're together she says she loves me and she spoons me after sex and she holds my hand when we walk to buy coffee in the morning. She's not interested in dating anyone. She's really busy. I don't tell her I love her because whenever I think about saying it, my hands twist up my stomach and wring it out. Then I'm left with this damp heavy tea towel inside me which festers a smell of sweet mold. Last night, Liat wasn't busy. I left my brother's place halfway through *Harold and Maude.* I felt her slimy teeth and taut lips on mine so we played a few rounds of "what," "nothing," giggle, lean in. Then she said, "Tell me what you want. Tell me the Truth." I scrunched up my nose. I took her words and put them inside this little box made of lead that's burried in my brain. Lead absorbs sound. Her breast fell into mine and I could feel her lips saying those same words on my neck. Silence hummed. My scowl loosened. I stared at her pink lit ceiling and tried to understand the shallow cracks. Cracks on the palm of her hands in the cold, or my hands in the cold. I didn't want to know more. She made her way down my torso. She scratched my thigh. Liat said something silly and I responded. Her hand pushed mine deeper into the mattress.

My forearms started to shake as more women dropped handfuls of gold bangles and gold earrings onto the gold platter I was holding. There were five of us with gold platters, maybe twenty-five women lined up before each of us. We were all dressed the same. Baggy pieces of earth toned fabric cocooned our bodies. Grey clouds swirled around the peak of a mountain. Lightning occasionally thrashed. One of the women told me she was hungry, one said that she "couldn't believe how long we'd been here." A tanned, tall woman with blue eyes and untamed eyebrows escorted me to a tent. She carried her platter with one hand and grabbed a bunch of the gold I'd collected with the other. She said she wished we were still slaves in Egypt. I replied, "Yeah . . . yeah Mount Sinai sucks." She smiled. In the tent we sorted the gold into piles. I wasn't too sure what the piles meant, but I started organising the gold according to size and no one told me I was wrong. I smacked my dry tongue against the roof of my mouth a few times and then asked the women where to get water. They laughed. I nibbled at my cuticles hoping to draw some wet blood as my eyes scanned the room. The gold piles glistened like the ocean in the sun so I shoved some earrings into my mouth. I swallowed them with ease. I shoved some more earrings and then some bangles. I sat down in the middle of the tent and grabbed handfuls of gold from whatever pile and shoved it all into my mouth. I heard one of the women say that the yetzer had entered me. I wasn't thirsty or hungry anymore, but I kept swallowing gold until all that was left were the golden platters, so I broke a platter into pieces and gnawed on a triangular segment like a lamb chop. I heard someone command, "strangle the yetzer." I went to grab another chunk of platter but my hands were sticky and red so I screamed and then I could smell roses and Rivkah's hair swallowed my face. I stopped screaming. She said my hands weren't bleeding. She kept holding me. She said we were at Milk Beach and it was January 18th. She repeated that a few times and rubbed my back. When I explained everything she scowled and said that doing acid was supposed be a break from wanting that kind of stuff.

Dew drops sparkled on the spider web that invited liberation. I enjoyed the familiar embrace, but silk strands turn to wagon ropes when damp words and feelings waterboard. Now life untangled never existed, and I write underwater. I wish I understood what my body felt like and what my mind dreamt of before rope cut me a waist.

Squirming in bed

like a wet leach covered in salt. Shaking into the fluffy soft you.

In the beginning, my body vibrates like a phone when it's first plugged in. Not from the vibrator's vibrating but because the silicon is freezing. Soon, the cold is inconsequential. I am distracted by people not really in my bed and actors not really on my phone. Sometimes the cold lingers. I think about how painful it would be to whack a tuning fork and rest it on my clit. I hate it when I think of someone fucking me who I would never want to really fuck. I press a button so the vibrating intensifies. I press it again. I imagine not having to imagine something realistic. Later in the night (unlike most nights) there is steam creeping up my window. There is warmth in my bed. I hope a stranger looks in from the street because this is what I really want even though his body feels a bit out of tune.

The soft cotton, frills, stuffing and zipper are loving and kind.

I think I like you better as a pillow.

For the

last month I've thought about Dan most days which makes my canines chew on these two little flaps inside my mouth. I should have predicted him leaving. Him not texting me since, because I haven't texted him. I've been sleeping more, visiting my family more. I messaged him a few days ago. I was hungover and the neighbour's dog was barking too loud. Ruth says he's a compulsive liar. We met and ate ice cream cross legged, facing each other. He had chocolate and I had lemon. He was telling me about his new place and how he already hated most of the housemates. I think I'm the only person he doesn't mind living with. He asked if I wanted to go to Tasmania with him soon, but I don't think it'll happen, and I'm not going to make it happen.' The little flaps inside my mouth started to sting. I instead attacked my orange ice cream spoon. He asked how the house was without him. "It's been clean but less fun." I bit too hard and the plastic spoon cracked in my mouth. I pulled it out and slit my lip. He dabbed the blood with his napkin and my mouth went limp. It was sweet. I was grateful. We caught the bus home.

'Maybe he'll make it happen, I should give him more credit.

To fill
the space that is ours
that I never wanted to fill.

To pour my self into the crusty shell they built for us.
I will leave next year.

To sulk like my mother,
I never wanted to pray
like my mother.

If a cockroach
crawled
over his toothbrush and
I saw,
he wouldn't want me to tell him.
As far as he knows, the toothbrush is clean and
only touched by him.

But if I saw a cockroach
crawl
over his toothbrush
every night for a week,
he would want me to tell him.

He knows it's unreasonable, but
he'd be angry with me.
He would say,
"Why didn't you tell me earlier?"

ב. To Receive

Two weeks after my twelfth birthday, I was gifted a lead box and three thousand dollars from my dead
grandmother's abusive husband.
He sat in a wheelchair, amputated leg exposed.
I delivered my dvar torah.
Mum drove around the block a few times.

He said I was blessed to inherit slender arms and
a rich bloodline.

"Was it good?"

"He was really
good."

"It felt
really good."

"The date was so
nice."

"He's so nice."

"I feel good about
this. It's all so nice."

"Rav Yitzhak bar Avdimi adds: This is a good trait in women, that they refrain from formulating their desire verbally."

—Eruvin 100b: 22. Babylonian Talmud.

דלא קא עביד איסורא. כשהוא יושב ואינו נותן הלאו דכל תגרע והעשה דונתן על קרנות נעקרין מאליהן אבל זה ישיבתו תשמיש הוא שהוא משתמש באילן: יכם. שאין בו נחלות ולאו מחובר הוא: בימות החמה. יכם מותר דליכא אפי׳ משום מראית העין שהרי ניכר לכל שהוא יכם שאינו מוליא עלין והא דקתני אסור בימות הגשמים שאין ניכר בין לח בין יכם ואיכא משום מראית העין: קא נתרי פירי. שנשארו בו משנה שעברה ואתי למשרי (א) ביה תלישה דלא נפי דעליה דיבש אטו עליה דלח לא גזרי׳ דהיא גופא גזירה מיהו תלישה אטו תלישה נגזר: בגדודא. יחור שנשרו ענפיו כולם:

לא קשיא הא בלחים הא ביבשים. וא״ת והא לעיל אמרינן ביבש דפרין והא נתרי קינסי כו׳ וי״ל דבאילן שהוא גבוה שייך למגזר טפי משום דמינכר ביה ניתרי קינסי: והאידנא דקי״ל כר״ש בולהו שרי. פי׳ ר״ח דהאי היתר לא קאי אלא אעשבים דשרי בכל ענין אבל באילן אין להוכיח שם שום היתר אפילו יבש דשייך למיגזר טפי משום דמנכרא מילתא: מיתיבי

I was wriggling my tube skirt back up my thighs when he turned on the lights and screamed "what the fuck." He ran downstairs. There was a cloud of blood on the white sheets. It was moving, pushed by the wind. The girls downstairs all said they only bled a little, a drop or something. I reached for the corner of the bed and pulled up the sheet. My friend had a mattress protector, it was stained but at least her mattress would be fine. I took all the bedding off and shoved it in her laundry basket. I stood up and almost fainted. It felt like a tiny Rabbi was leading the Viddui inside my skull. כזבנו לצנו מרדנו. I stuck my shaking fingers down my throat and watched beige liquid fall into her en suite toilet. I cried after that, but I always cry after I vomit. I wet a hand towel and wiped between my legs. Once Rivkah left a bloody hand towel next to our toilet at home so I barged into her room whilst her friend was over and told her to clean up her period mess. She squeezed my arm and led me to the bathroom. I didn't realise it would embarrass her so much. I wrapped the now pink hand towel in amongst the bloody sheets. I put on more mascara. If my eyelashes were a person, they'd have great posture. Ruth was walking up the stairs when I was heading down. She squeezed my arm and pulled me back to the bedroom. Apparently his white shirt was covered in blood. The shirt was expensive, he slammed the front door when he left. Her dry hands rubbed my bare thighs. She was much more tanned than me, I liked the shape of her nails. Almond. I told her I orgasmed. "Rivkah said she also bled a lot. It means his dick is big. I don't know why he's mad. This probably happens to him all the time." We chuckled, and it felt like an electric drill was being shoved up my vagina and through my uterus. תעבנו תעינו. I strike my chest for the last time. I lower my hands to either side of my hips. Mum's cheeks have silver tear trails like the residue a snail leaves behind. We sit. Her hand rests on my shaking thigh. I turn to Rivkah and whisper how sorry I am for asking her to clean up her bloody towel. She says she doesn't remember. She's sorry I walked in on her when I was seven.

I lay there with my mouth limp and let the heavy man continue to kiss me. The concrete crushed against my shoulders. Hands by my side. The thought of leaving swirled around my mind like his wet tongue in my mouth. He was too heavy, I was too tired. I let him jam his cold fingers up me. I threw away the undies I wore that night.

הגהות הב״ח

גליון הש״ס

מוסף רש״י

My body felt like a sigh. Light. Invisible. Sleepy. A long sigh that glides slowly through the air without a purpose. He asked me if I came. I did, so I told him. He said it was the first time he had ever made a girl cum. I was still floating. His words passed me by without much regard. He asked me if I really came. Then he asked me if I was lying, because he knows often girls do. He asked me again if I was lying. I think he asked me another time too. I told the truth, but he couldn't hear it. He couldn't see me. So I floated around his room looking for leverage. He folded his underwear and hung all of his t-shirts. He just had stationary in his desk draws. He called my name probably assuming I went to the toilet. He called it again, longer and louder. Then he yawned and I dived into his mouth and fell into his stomach. I screamed my name too but heard only the gurgling of his digestive system.

He saw hair that would
1. whiten the crow drizzle down my neck. He imagined a fringe like Salomé, a turban like
2. Rachel. He pushed back and forth and shook the bells amongst my curls. The crows that
3. perch on the grey roofs at Majdanek kept the prettiest for the end. Kept me further from
4. where she resides. Suffocated by splinters, I
5. lay beneath You on the seventh day - created by the man who painted my hair with blue ink.
6. Hair long like Lilit, You wrote. Deaf and
7. blind awaiting my return. The time went, You don't know how.

לעזי רש״י

רב ניסים גאון

When I was eleven I looked down the deepest hole in Jerusalem. The exhibit had a few lights near the top but most of the hole was subsumed in shadows. I was intimidated by its depth but could not really observe it. Besides diagrams and porn, Liv's was the first vagina I'd seen. It was ashy, glazed by a smokescreen. I couldn't know it's depth, history, what it was supposed to mean to me. I think my vagina has nothing deep about it. A rational vagina, always cast in clinical lighting. "Your tongues too timid" she told me later that night. "And your hands are too shy." She grabbed my fringe right near the scalp and pulled my head up. She told me to touch with integrity. I said integrity isn't the same as going hard, and she said, "But strength is honesty. Just hold the whole of me." She grinned and caressed my cheek as if she was begining to uncover what she herself was.

A wedged doorstop weighs on my tongue. The slant steepens when my jaw opens. If I tilt my head back, it slides down my throat. It jabs splinters into my tonsils. It stifles my demands before they swing out.

We walked around to the driveway together holding hands. Our fingers didn't interlock or anything, it was more like a long sweaty handshake. My knees stung from the jagged gravel. My left knee more than my right because the driveway was slanted. He pushed my head back and forth like a kid on a swing. I always hated going too high. My stomach would clench and my eyes would water. I wanted to stop. I stood up. He begged me to keep going. He said it would hurt otherwise. He said it didn't affect me to keep going, now that I'd already started. He asked what he did wrong. I started to cry. He grabbed my forearms and told me that he didn't mean to make me cry. Then he hugged me, so I stopped crying. He did up his pants. He apologised. I walked back inside clasping my own hands, interlocking my fingers. The hallway looked halated, like some first-time director had covered my eyeballs in vaseline to shoot a sultry short film. My knees were dotted with pink imprints. I headed straight to the bathroom and washed my hands three times. The soap smelt like lavender. I wished it was something stronger, maybe lime. The smell of penis stained the back of my throat. This one time Rivkah and I drove to a picnic with a pear and blue cheese salad. It was freezing outside so we kept the windows up, the whole car filled with a similar tasting stain. His friends were my friends. We had a few options. One, pretend like this never happened. Two, continue doing whatever this is until he decides it's over. Three, we could date. He kissed me goodbye that night in front of everyone. I understood what had been chosen. A few weeks later he slept in my bed, and I watched the ceiling fan.

Mum always told me how much she liked my first boyfriend. He was shomer negiah except with me, but I was pretty sure that wasn't allowed. He went to synagogue every shabbat. He said I had to let him kiss me. He couldn't hug other girls. Mum told me not to tell my friends at school. It might turn one of them anti-Semitic.

Dan brought me tea the next morning. He always offered me tea when I had my period. I'm not sure who taught him that. I told him who I got with last night. We laughed and it felt natural.

When I told Dan what actually happened, he said I must call the now lame and heavy man (we can't say his name anymore) and tell him what he did to me. "You know humans learnt modesty from the cat which covers it's shit, and monogamy from the dove who is faithful to its partner." If the lame and heavy man learns what he did was wrong, he hopefully won't do it again. Dan said I must never talk to the lame and heavy man at parties. I burnt my tongue on the rose tea. I kept sipping, drinking at least half whilst too hot.

דלא קא עביד איסורא אבל הכא דקא עביד איסורא הכי נמי דירד תני חדא אחד אילן לח ואחד אילן יבש ותניא אידך בד"א בלח אבל ביבש מותר אמר רב יהודה ל"ק כאן בשגוזע מחליף כאן בשאין גוזע מחליף גוזע מחליף יבש קרית ליה אלא לא קשיא כאן בימות החמה כאן בימות הגשמים בימות החמה הא נתרי פירי בדליכא פירי והא קא נתרי קניסי בגרודרא איני והא רב איקלע לאפסטיא ואסר בגרודא רב בקעה מצא וגדר בה גדר: אמר רמי בר אבא אמר רב

מיתיבי

אסי אסור לאדם שיהלך על גבי עשבים בשבת משום שנאמר ואץ ברגלים חוטא תני חדא מותר לילך ע"ג עשבים בשבת ותניא אידך אסור ל"ק הא בלחים הא ביבשים ואי בעית אימא הא והא בלחים ולא קשיא כאן בימות החמה כאן בימות הגשמים ואיבעית אימא הא והא בימות החמה ול"ק הא דסיים מסאניה הא דלא סיים מסאניה ואיבעית אימא הא והא דסיים מסאניה ול"ק הא דאית ליה עוקצי הא דלית ליה עוקצי ואיבעית אימא הא והא דאית ליה עוקצי הא דאית ליה שרכא הא דלית ליה שרכא והאידנא דקיימא לן כר"ש כולהו שרי: ואמר רמי בר חמא אמר רב אסי אסור לאדם שיכוף אשתו לדבר מצוה שנאמר ואץ ברגלים חוטא ואר"י יהושע בן לוי כל הכופה אשתו לדבר מצוה הויין לו בנים שאינן מהוגנין אמר רב איקא בר חיננא מאי קראה גם בלא דעת נפש לא טוב תניא נמי הכי גם בלא דעת נפש לא טוב זה הכופה אשתו לדבר מצוה ואץ ברגלים חוטא זה הבועל ושונה איני והאמר רבא הרוצה לעשות כל בניו זכרים יבעול וישנה ל"ק כאן לדעת כאן שלא לדעת: א"ר שמואל בר נחמני א"ר יוחנן כל אשה שתובעת בעלה לדבר מצוה הווין לה בנים שאפילו בדורו של משה לא היו כמותן דאילו בדורו של משה כתיב הבו לכם אנשים חכמים ונבונים וידועים לשבטיכם וכתיב ואקח את ראשי שבטיכם אנשים חכמים וידועים ואילו נבונים לא אשכח ואילו גבי לאה כתיב ותצא לאה לקראתו ותאמר אלי תבוא כי שכר שכרתיך וכתיב ומבני יששכר יודעי בינה לעתים לדעת מה יעשה ישראל ראשיהם מאתים וכל אחיהם על פיהם איני והאמר רב יצחק בר אבדימי עשר קללות נתקללה חוה דכתיב אל האשה אמר הרבה ארבה אלו שני טפי דמים אחת דם נדה ואחת דם בתולים עצבונך זה צער גידול בנים והרונך זה צער העיבור בעצב תלדי בנים כמשמעו ואל אישך תשוקתך מלמד שהאשה משתוקקת על בעלה בשעה שיוצא לדרך והוא ימשל בך מלמד שהאשה תובעת בלב והאיש תובע בפה זו היא מדה טובה בנשים כי קאמרינן דמרציא ארצויי קמיה הני שבע הווין כי אתא רב דימי אמר עטופה כאבל ומנודה מכל אדם וחבושה בבית האסורין מאי מנודה מכל אדם אילימא משום דאסיר לה יחוד איהו נמי אסיר ליה יחוד אלא דאסירא לבי תרי במתניתא תנא מגדלת שער כלילית ויושבת ומשתנת מים כבהמה ונעשית כר לבעלה ואידך הני שבח הוא לה דא"ר חייא מאי דכתיב מלפנו מבהמות ארץ ומעוף השמים יחכמנו מלפנו מבהמות זו פרידה שכורעת ומשתנת מים ומעוף השמים יחכמנו זה תרנגול שמפייס ואחר כך בועל אמר רבי יוחנן אילמלא לא ניתנה תורה היינו למידין צניעות מחתול וגזל מנמלה ועריות מיונה דרך ארץ מתרנגול שמפייס ואחר כך בועל ומאי מפייס לה אמר רב יהודה אמר רב הכי קאמר לה זבינגא ליך זיגא דמטו ליך עד כרעיך לבתר הכי אמר לה לישמטתיה לכרבלתיה דההוא תרנגולא אי אית ליה ולא זבינגא ליך:

מתני'

תורה אור השלם

1. גם בלא דעת נפש לא טוב ואץ ברגלים חוטא: משלי יט ב
2. הבו לכם אנשים חכמים ונבנים וידעים לשבטיכם ואשימם בראשיכם: דברים א יג
3. ואקח את ראשי שבטיכם אנשים חכמים וידעים ואתן אתם ראשים עליכם שרי אלפים ושרי מאות ושרי חמשים ושרי עשרת ושטרים לשבטיכם: דברים א טו
4. ויבא יעקב מן השדה בערב ותצא לאה לקראתו ותאמר אלי תבוא כי שכר שכרתיך בדודאי בני וישכב עמה בלילה הוא: בראשית ל טז
5. ומבני יששכר יודעי בינה לעתים לדעת מה יעשה ישראל ראשיהם מאתים וכל אחיהם על פיהם: דברי הימים א יב לג
6. אל האשה אמר הרבה ארבה עצבונך והרנך בעצב תלדי בנים ואל אישך תשוקתך והוא ימשל בך: בראשית ג טז
7. מלפנו מבהמות ארץ ומעוף השמים יחכמנו: איוב לה יא

לעזי רש"י

[illegible]

רב נסים גאון

[illegible]

רבינו חננאל

[illegible]

[illegible]

Kmart shuffling in the
suffering he called inevitable when my quick thumbs cheapened the travail of listening and comforting. Cold sweat for her sorrow and my social strategising. His parking ticket. I've got coins. Should have sent a voice note.

אל האשה אמר הרבה
ארבה, אלו שני טפי דמים — אחת דם נדה, ואחת דם בתולים. עצבונך, זה צער גידול בנים. והרונך, זה צער העיבור. בעצב תלדי בנים, כמשמעו. ואל אישך תשוקתך, מלמד שהאשה משתוקקת על בעלה בשעה שיוצא לדרך. והוא ימשל בך, מלמד שהאשה תובעת בלב והאיש תובע בפה.

ג. To Forgive

Hold my figs

in your

hands.

Raw,

pulsating,

bloody.

Before they turn blue, remember them

growing on the tree you planted in me

after we

read Plath and

booked flights to Berlin.

Rinse my figs in a public bathroom sink.

And please remember this offering because it's not
worth diving on a sword if you forget that I
did it
for you.
(I think about how good it feels
to fall and forget where I'm landing.) The tiled floor
freezes
my soles and toes.

When you return my figs, I'll wear them around my neck
so you do not forget how I gave you
everything I could.

"Reish Lakish said: Great is repentance, as the penitent's intentional sins are counted for him as unwitting transgressions, as it is stated: 'Return, Israel, to the Lord your God, for you have stumbled in your iniquity' (Hosea 14:2). The Gemara analyzes this: Doesn't 'iniquity' mean an intentional sin? Yet the prophet calls it stumbling, implying that one who repents is considered as though he only stumbled accidentally in his transgression. The Gemara asks: Is that so? Didn't Reish Lakish himself say: Great is repentance, as one's intentional sins are counted for him as merits, as it is stated: 'And when the wicked turns from his wickedness, and does that which is lawful and right, he shall live thereby' (Ezekiel 33:19), and all his deeds, even his transgressions, will become praiseworthy?"

—Yoma 86b. The Babylonian Talmud

unwitting

God

in

your

stumbling,

Great

as

wickedness

which

shall

become

praiseworthy.

(א) אמר ר' יוחנן גדולה תשובה שדוחה את לא תעשה שבתורה שנאמר לאמר הן ישלח איש את אשתו והלכה מאתו והיתה לאיש אחר הישוב אליה עוד הלא חנוף תחנף הארץ ההיא ואת זנית רעים רבים ושוב אלי נאם ה' א"ר יונתן גדולה תשובה (ב)(שמקרבת) את הגאולה שנאמר ובא לציון גואל ולשבי פשע ביעקב מה טעם ובא לציון גואל משום דשבי פשע ביעקב אמר ריש לקיש גדולה תשובה שזדונות נעשות לו כשגגות שנאמר שובה ישראל עד ה' אלהיך כי כשלת בעונך הא עון מזיד הוא וקא קרי ליה מכשול איני והאמר ריש לקיש גדולה תשובה שזדונות נעשות לו כזכיות שנאמר ובשוב רשע מרשעתו ועשה משפט וצדקה עליהם (חיה) יחיה לא קשיא כאן מאהבה כאן מיראה אמר ר' שמואל בר נחמני אמר ר' יונתן גדולה תשובה שמארכת (ג) שנותיו של אדם שנאמר ובשוב רשע מרשעתו (חיו) יחיה אמר ר' יצחק אמרי במערבא משמיה דרבה בר מרי בא וראה שלא כמדת הקדוש ברוך הוא מדת בשר ודם מקניט את חבירו (ג) בדברים ספק מתפיים הימנו ספק אין מתפיים הימנו וא"ת מתפיים הימנו ספק מתפיים (ד) בדברים ספק אין מתפיים בדברים אבל הקב"ה אדם עובר עבירה בסתר מתפיים ממנו בדברים שנאמר קחו עמכם דברים ושובו אל ה' ולא עוד אלא שמחזיק לו טובה שנאמר וקח טוב ולא עוד אלא שמעלה עליו הכתוב כאילו הקריב פרים שנאמר ונשלמה פרים שפתינו שמא תאמר פרי חובה ת"ל ארפא משובתם אוהבם נדבה תניא היה ר"מ אומר גדולה תשובה שבשביל יחיד שעשה תשובה מוחלין (ה) לכל העולם כולו שנא' ארפא משובתם אוהבם נדבה כי שב אפי ממנו מהם לא נאמר אלא ממנו היכי דמי בעל תשובה אמר רב יהודה כגון שבאת לידו דבר עבירה פעם ראשונה ושניה (ו) וניצל הימנה מחוי רב יהודה באותה אשה באותו פרק באותו מקום א"ר יהודה רב רמי כתיב אשרי נשוי פשע כסוי חטאה וכתיב מכסה פשעיו לא יצליח לא קשיא הא בחטא מפורסם הא בחטא שאינו מפורסם רב זוטרא בר טוביה אמר רב נחמן כאן בעבירות שבין אדם לחבירו כאן בעבירות שבין אדם למקום תניא ר' יוסי בר יהודה אומר אדם עובר עבירה פעם ראשונה מוחלין לו שניה מוחלין לו שלישית מוחלין לו רביעית אין מוחלין לו שנאמר כה אמר ה' על שלשה פשעי ישראל ועל ארבעה לא אשיבנו (ונאמר) הן כל אלה יפעל אל פעמים שלש עם גבר מאי ואומר וכי תימא הני מילי בציבור אבל ביחיד לא ת"ש הן כל אלה יפעל אל פעמים שלש עם גבר (מכאן ואילך אין מוחלין לו שנאמר על שלשה פשעי ישראל ועל ארבעה לא אשיבנו) ת"ר עבירות שהתודה עליהן יוה"כ זה לא יתודה עליהן יום הכפורים אחר ואם שנה בהן צריך להתודות יוה"כ אחר ואם לא שנה בהן וחזר והתודה עליהן עליו הכתוב אומר ככלב שב על קיאו כסיל שונה באולתו רבי אליעזר בן יעקב אומר כ"ש שהוא משובח שנאמר כי פשעי אני אדע וחטאתי נגדי תמיד אלא מה אני מקיים ככלב שב על קיאו וגו' כדרב הונא דאמר רב הונא כיון שעבר אדם עבירה ושנה בה הותרה לו הותרה לו סלקא דעתך אלא אימא נעשית לו כהיתר וצריך לפרוט את החטא שנאמר אנא חטא העם הזה חטאה גדולה ויעשו להם אלהי זהב דברי ר' יהודה בן בבא רבי עקיבא אומר (ז) אשרי נשוי פשע כסוי חטאה אלא מהו שאמר משה ויעשו להם אלהי זהב כדר' ינאי דאמר ר' ינאי אמר משה לפני הקדוש ברוך הוא רבש"ע כסף וזהב שהרבית להם לישראל עד שאמרו די גרם להם שיעשו אלהי זהב שני פרנסים טובים עמדו להם לישראל משה ודוד משה אמר יכתב סורחני שנאמר יען לא האמנתם בי להקדישני דוד אמר אל יכתב סורחני שנאמר אשרי נשוי פשע כסוי חטאה משל דמשה ודוד למה הדבר דומה לשתי נשים שלקו בבית דין אחת קלקלה ואחת אכלה פגי שביעית אמרה להן אותה שאכלה פגי שביעית בבקשה מכם הודיעו על מה היא לוקה שלא יאמרו על מה שזו לוקה זו לוקה הביאו פגי שביעית ותלו בצוארה והיו מכריזין לפניה ואומרין על עסקי שביעית היא לוקה מפרסמין את החנפין מפני חילול השם שנאמר ובשוב צדיק מצדקו ועשה עול ונתתי מכשול לפניו תשובת המוחלטין מעכבת הפורענות ואע"פ שנחתם עליו גזר דין של פורענות שלות רשעים סופה תקלה והרשות מקברת את בעליה ערום נכנס לה וערום יצא ממנה ולואי שתהא יציאה כביאה רב כי הוה נפיק למידן דינא אמר הכי בצבו נפשיה לקטלא נפיק וצבו ביתיה לית הוא עביד וריקן לביתיה אזיל ולואי שתהא ביאה (ח) כיציאה רבא כי הוה נפיק לדינא אמר הכי בצבו

רש"י

לא תעשה שבתורה. לא יוכל בעלה הראשון וגו': כי כשלת בעונך. עונך יחשב כמכשול שהיא שגגה: עליהם (חיו) [הוא] יחיה. על כל מה שעשה ואף על העבירות: מתפיים הימנו. מקבל הימנו פיוסים: ונשלמה פרים שפתינו. במקום פרים: נדבה. מקובלת ברצון יותר מחובה: ארפא משובתם. (ט) מן היחיד: שבא דבר עבירה לידו. (י) שנכשל בה כבר: באותה אשה באותו מקום. שעבר שם (כ) העבירה ואותו פרק מתוך שדומה מכל וכל לזמן שנכשל בו כבר יצרו מתגבר עליו ואומר לו ראה פלונית ואותו מקום ואותו פרק הוא קום עשה מה שעשית כבר: כסוי חטאה. שלא נתגלה עונו: בחטא מפורסם. טוב לו שיודה ויתבייש ולא יכפור בו: בחטא שאינו מפורסם. לא יגלה חטאו וכבוד השם הוא שכל מה שאדם חוטא כפרהסיא מיעוט כבוד שמים הוא: עבירות שבין אדם לחבירו. יגלה לרבים שיבקשו ממנו שימחול לו: וחטאתי נגדי תמיד. איני סבור שכפרת לי והרי הוא תמיד כאילו הוא נגדי עומד: וצריך לפרט את החטא. כשהוא מתודה אומר חטא פלוני חטאתי: כדר' ינאי. לא הזכיר העון אלא למעטו ולומר אתה גרמת להם משל (ק) לאדם שהיה לו בן נאה ומאכילו ומשקהו ותולה לו כיס של דינרין בצוארו והושיבו בפתח זונות מה יעשה שלא יחטא: הכי גרס בספרי משה אמר יכתב סורחני שנאמר יען לא האמנתם בי. בכל מקום שנכתב מיתתו שם נכתב סרחונו. אלמא ניחא למכתביה ומנין טובא: לשתי נשים. שלוקות: אחת קלקלה. זנתה והתרו בה למלקות כך דור המדבר מתו במדבר שהאמינו למרגלים ר) (משה) מת במדבר על שמעו נא המורים אמר יכתב סורחני שלא יאמרו אף אני קלקלתי כמותם: פגי שביעית. תאנים שלא בישלו כל צרכן ורחמנא אמר והיתה שבת הארץ לכם לאכלה (ויקרא כה) לאכלה ולא להפסד: מפרסמין את החנפין. שהן רשעים ומראין עצמן כצדיקים אם יש מכיר במעשיו מצוה לפרסמו מפני חילול השם שבני אדם למידין ממעשיו שסבורין עליו שהוא צדיק ועוד כשבא עליו פורענות בני אדם אומרים מה הועיל לו זכותו: שנאמר ובשוב צדיק מצדקו. סיפיה דקרא ונתתי מכשול לפניו אני ממציא לידו חטא גלוי לכל שיכשל בו וידעו את מעשיו: המוחלטין. רשעים גמורין: שלות רשעים סופה תקלה. מתוך שלותם הם יושבין ומהרהרין בעבירות: והרשות. הרבנות: מקברת בעליה. שנאמר (שמות א) וימת יוסף תחילה ואח"כ כל אחיו ש): ולואי שתהא יציאה. ממנה בלא חטא כביאה: נפיק לדינא. להיות דן דין:

מוסף רש"י

רבינו חננאל

גליון הש"ס

הגהות הב"ח

תוס' ישנים

It was a piercing sting. The red handprint on my arm was screeching. My eyes welled over with tears, but I didn't sulk. I still left with him slept in his bed, let him spoon me in the morning, kept the itchy woolen blanket perched between our bare skin and hid from the sunlight that peaked through his venetian blinds. I forgave him a week later which was the last time we spoke about it.

I didn't mind paying for most meals. It was all temporary. I knew we would break up in January.

He'd said, "If I ever did anything to make your life harder last year, I'm really sorry." I wasn't going to break eye contact. He smelt like shit. I tried to swallow a chuckle but ended up spraying little flicks of spit onto his face. His eyes were so brown, oozing with genuine remorse. The house was almost empty. He moved in two months ago. This was the longest we've spoken one on one. I was precariously holding my bed side table and it was jabbing my stomach. I just wanted to get to my car. I smiled kindly, "No, no everything's fine." My bedside table fit in the backseat which was almost full of my smaller furniture. Maybe he's just sorry because he broke up with his girlfriend a few days ago. Or maybe he realised that apologising can instantly rid someone of blame.

And then everything was fine

Cold sheets jammed in between my calf and thigh, unwitting prayers shoved into the kotel. I gulped down whatever saliva remained in my always dry mouth. My throat hurt. It's the beginning of winter.

Rivkah wouldn't leave my room until the trade was complete. She slouched on the edge of my bed. I wriggled further away from her. The room smells like roses whenever she's in it. She buys nice perfume that I'm not allowed to use. Rivkah believes that to receive an apology one must make themselves available. I apologised, and it was like sculling water with stevia mixed in it. She forgave me quickly only to make sure that next time I'd do the same for her. She doesn't seem to care if I mean what I say or not. I don't think she can tell the difference.

Ruth told me he's a dog who eats his own vomit. I think that makes me the vomit. She said that's not what she meant, but I should cut him off already. I'd let Dan live with me again. Let him finger me again. Let him scratch my car again and let him tell me he didn't scratch my car again. He was a God to me again. On our last night in the apartment, we got high and watched *Survivor*. I wriggled down the couch and curled into fetal position, tucked my cold feet into his front left jean pocket. He giggled and started to massage my ankles. He apologised for letting himself leave me stranded, again. The sweat on my hand became thick and chunky like PVA glue. Dan wagged his tail and barked. I could only feel happy for him.

Mum's dark brown curls faded into the sky behind us. She wrapped up, "Who am I to complain. You know, there are people who have it so much worse off than me. I'm, fine." Under my breath I mumbled amen and pictured a chorus of ten women crowded around two flickering candles in the courtyard of our shule singing, "Baruch atah adonai, I'm fine." These women kept repeating the prayer, eyes covered by each hand, shyly bowing. Eloheinu I'm fine, melech ha'olam I'm fine, lehadlik ner shel I'm fine. I coldly told mum to see a psychologist. She looked to the sky and blinked a lot, then dabbed her wet eyes and face with her fingertips. I picked at my cuticles. She slowed her stumbling breath when Sam and Reuben joined us on the balcony. She smiled to them. I was surprised when mum started seeing Sam again. Last she had told me, he was with Petra. They slumped on the blue and white striped couch opposite us. Such an ugly outdoor furniture set. Sam continued explaining how his new company makes their Great Meat Pies. You have to pump the cooked meat into the frozen pastry shells. He rolled a cigarette with one hand and offered me a sip of his bourbon with the other. I'm not sure why he offered. I've never accepted. From my left thumb, I tweezed out a wick and squeezed below the nail, drawing blood. I stuck my thumb into my mouth. It tingled and warmed up. Sam and Reuben moved on to discuss feminisms irrelevance in our "current context" as mum said something about how cute I looked with my thumb in my mouth. I shuffled closer and rested my head on her shoulder. She began to whisper fears disguised as apologies. Like gum that would never disintegrate, they landed at the bottom of my stomach. She didn't want to be like her mother. She was scared of burdening me with her problems. Before I could respond, Sam asked me to get him another drink and maybe "that sweet sesame thing, if we have it." Mum quickly nudged me to fix my face's wickedness. If I accepted or refused his request, it wouldn't bother him. He wasn't born with fear. It didn't coerce him to believe in God, just in case God does exist. It would never push him off balance and then grab him by the neck like that one time I came home from school and saw mum painting our kitchen purple. Purple paint on the cupboards, the fridge, in her hair. Fear would never follow his grandmother from Europe on a fake passport that now hides at the bottom of his pyjama drawer. He can see other people for who they are, not for who they are because of all the ways he's fucked them up. He stretched out his arm and rubbed mum's knees affectionately. She smiled again. He quickly winked. I wiped my wet thumb on my jeans and sprung off the couch. I told her everything was fine. I know she is fine, and I'm fine too. Amen.

I wish I had never said that I couldn't be with you for more than ten minutes at a time, and I wish I could go back to tell him that you're actually good at packing instead of saying you always overpack.

I didn't say the right things to the lame and heavy man. We sat in a loud bar and he ordered us drinks. I told him I hate my job. He told me he loves his job. He told me he was in a weird place last month. I said I understand and that I liked his shirt. He ordered us pizza. I didn't trust the prawns.

He cried and repeatedly told me it's not his fault that his grandparents were nazis. My chest was cold from his tears and dribble. I sporadically ran my fingers through his soft, thin hair. The sky was only black. I don't think much was black at Majdanek. I just remember grey and brown and crows which seemed to recognise me. Sex with him was always bland, but I'm glad I've now seen an uncircumcised penis in real life. I told him my friends can be too insensitive. "Classic Jewish humour," he said, "guilt shouldn't be so funny." I could hear Ruth cackling inside. I thought about pinning him to the concrete floor and carving a swastika into his forehead, *Inglorious Basterds* style. I had my keys on me. For a moment I felt ashamed for thinking such violent thoughts. He's not actually a nazi, but shall I slash his jugular with a chalif like how the shochet kills the chickens? Slice his carotid arteries, vagus nerve, trachea, and then he wouldn't be in pain. I stared at his bare neck that rested near my heart. He explained that he forgives me because it's not my fault that my friends are bitches, "You know, just like how it's not my fault that my grandparents had to become nazis." I told him it was a little different because I got to choose my friends, so technically, I'm more horrible. He laughed and wiped his nose on my shirt.

I scattered ripped up chunks of stale white baguette and threw them into the pond already full of bread from the students. I forgave myself for not having achieved any of the goals thirteen year old me repeated every night before bed. I needed to be praiseworthy.

Last two panadols gulped down
the empty sheet's in the bin.

An exit the same as an entrance
can't be for that which serves a purpose.

No matter how much we rearrange the living room,
cover the walls with collages
and the couches with crocheted blankets,
we both know all that happened.
The difference is I'm not hurt.

Acknowledgments

This book was a finalist in *The Hunger*'s Tiny Fork Chapbook Series 2021 contest.

The first iteration of part of this work first appeared in *Voiceworks* Issue 122.

Much of this chapbook came together while studying at the University of Sydney. Julia Cooper Clark and Mark Peart, thank you for the guidance.

Thank you, eternally, to my mum Orli for the discussions, support, and unconditional love. Rodney, Gidon, and Leah—thank you as well, love you.

YAEL GRUNSEIT (she/her) is a writer and filmmaker hailing from unceded Eora land (Sydney, Australia). Since moving to New York, Yael has been studying film directing at the Feirstein Graduate School of Cinema. Her previous writing projects can be found in Voiceworks and Shirley Magazine. Her latest zine *Facing Each Other In Silence For Too Long* was printed at Small Editions and can be found at *Fiend*.

www.ingramcontent.com/pod-product-compliance
Lightning Source LLC
Chambersburg PA
CBHW081509040426
42446CB00017B/3447
* 9 7 8 1 9 5 7 2 4 8 0 9 7 *